CHARGE

Leigh Faulkner

Published by Fiddlehead Poetry Books, Fredericton, N.B., 1982, with the assistance of The University of New Brunswick and The Canada Council.

© Leigh Faulkner, 1982

Cover design by Jennifer Hunt

Canadian Cataloguing Publication Data

Faulkner, Leigh.
  Charge

Poems.

ISBN 0-86492-020-2

I. Title.

PS8561.A94C52	C811'.54	C82-094892-6
PR9199.3.F3852		

CONTENTS

I

Nightfall Over Pugwash River
Canticle: In Darkness the Powers Gather
A White Mold Lengthens
Fall on the LaHave
Forerunners
The Dark Hours

II

The Tantramar
Suddenly I Am Aware of the Sky
Elegy
In One Extreme Cell
Approaching the Well
Charge

III

Fear of Dark Things
Midnight
Amoroso
The Lover
To Inanna
Avatar

— *For Edna*

I

NIGHTFALL OVER PUGWASH RIVER

leaves roll edges away from the sky
it is night by the river
shore birds have curled into themselves

the dull sun still shines in eyes
setting far back among wind dunes
leaping and candle-falling

a long hand is closing on naked breasts
and owls moan under dark eastern stone
alive to black milk cold in their beaks

painfully time has been stopped at this point
and images gathered by a child's mirror
fall out
are broken

like stars on the water

CANTICLE: IN DARKNESS THE POWERS GATHER

moose move down to the saltwater
to rid themselves of blood-divining ticks
and each noonday
the sun is higher

dusty backroads
reach across their ditches
and smother bushes and ferns

what is laughter in these times?

middle-earth closes:
the machine grinds on

in darkness
the powers gather . . .

a silver bird flutters in anguish,
its throat song-swollen

A WHITE MOLD LENGTHENS

The swift, sweet wind
fallen from the north,
squirrels' calls
extinguished among the leaves and upper branches;
among the mosses,
silence.

A white mold
lengthens
in the half-formed humus;
a late larva
bristles with wings
in the frog-spit on a fiddlehead.

Silence and wings:
the dichotomy of excellence.

FALL ON THE LAHAVE

It's October now
and the fish hawks have left
the river.

All summer
I watched them,
at first perplexed by the tenuous bat cries,
always awed by their needlepoint artistry of death.

The mink is bolder in October,
almost disdainful as it circles the little cove
from the silted lobster boat hulk
to the scrubby eel-grass marsh
to its home in the timbers and rocks of my neighbour's wharf.

Only the carrion eaters,
the crows and gulls,
are unchanged,
as black and white.

FORERUNNERS

the clearing's cupped hands
hold back the night's
bone and saliva

only small concussions
touch my tent,
mapping
feathers
and a faintly opaque furrow
through the new-fall veneer of pine needles —
prey
I will hunt in the morning
after the sun eases each stoma,
pries insects from the trees' coarse scales
and thick dark from among trunks and branches

THE DARK HOURS

A bird flutters in the mind,
tangled in a lacework of stars;
the tiny worm carried from birth
spirals out to the eye
and curls unnoticed on the edge of the retina
to become, in time, the beast
that will be ridden into eternity,
ridden until one spring it falls exhausted

and the rider,
thankful,
slides off into the long grass
and feels once again the moist earth
and the deep impression made a lifetime before . . .

In the emptiness of bed
it takes no hammer
to break illusions.

Here, the snow
scuffing the window,
I sit up,
tending the fire,
intent that the wind
shall not find me asleep
during the dark hours.

II

THE TANTRAMAR
— in memory of John Thompson

Darkness spills from the long roots of the marsh grass
And rises, filling the broken barns;
Night, thick as old blood,
Presses into the hills;
Slick-furred animals with empty bellies
Move along the edges of the salt ponds;
The moment of wind-change arrives
And the mists hang motionless.

It's a place few leave easily —
The mud on kodiaks and wool jacket
Brushes off
In dark images and words:
A shotgun shell
Lying on the kitchen table in April;
A book of Yeats,
And one of Ghalib.

There were evenings of beer and cigarettes,
Beethoven and Piaf —
Evenings when our poems
Were full of the northwind
And geese gathering over the Tantramar
For the hard flight
Away . . .
And there were pauses in our poems
While we listened to the poetry in their cries . . .

SUDDENLY I AM AWARE OF THE SKY

Suddenly I am aware of the sky:
clouds
        drawn across the full moon
                into the eastern vortex

If the wind ceased,
would I still
        worship?
Still breathe poems?

Remember child-songs? —
Sibelius,
      his uneasy power so troubling
like slaughter-houses raised on the farms of friends
or wild swans
        flightless

There is a beating like drums in the blood —
strength
      rising
    like Goya's Colossus
and darkness leaving,
following the clouds into the east

ELEGY

winter's white fire
like the acute hunger
of the child within
encloses me

I reach toward sleep
and my thin fingers
grow down through the bed
the floor
and stroke animals
awaiting the libation of spring

through thick fur
I feel that moment approaching
shaking the firmly rooted grass and trees
scattering frost sparks —

the glow of things near and beautiful

luxuriant flames
flooding from the mouths of creatures
awakening to share this weight
they have carried so long

IN ONE EXTREME CELL

winter:
    rigid,
        sharp-cornered

melted today
in one extreme cell
of the maple outside my window

in one cell of the highest twig
the fluid melted
and the convection currents
stroked the nucleus
into sub-molecular vibration

once more the sun crossed a line
and watchers took note

already the design for a nest
is forming in a robin's eye

APPROACHING THE WELL

there have been blood sacrifices
in the east this morning

here
grass that gave reality to the sun
holds the sky in its stiffness

burdened by this cold
I go out to the well

and find darkness
seeping from the deep rock
the smoothness of new ice

against this there is no defence

I raise my hands
feel the sun like flint
strike fire from my nails

a brief flaming of stars
that lightens the necessity of day

CHARGE

turn:
    feel space press

        my dark forest
        parts before knife-eyed hunters
        I call by name

whose bones? —
    a childhood moment has lasting weight;
    I ache to rest though there are things
    I am not asked to carry

at night I am an ant:
    so it is I chew delicate roots
    and venture to the sleeping place of the fieldmouse

not even my wife knows my love of silence

III

FEAR OF DARK THINGS

How we fear darkness:
Turn away from deep water,
Light fires at sunset;
                    I'm not one
Who has loved often:
                         Love
Is dark
And has great weight —
                       like suicide;
It annihilates,
          like night fog,
All but the deepest sounds;
How we fear darkness:
Love,
Poems about love;
We fear both of these.

MIDNIGHT

The lingering moment is drawn away
By the black snow,
By the bell;
Old men turn from their windows.

They do not see the lovers with warm eyes
Rising from the snow.

AMOROSO

I'm asleep in my blood,
like a bird curled under the moon;
the wine of your love
is strong

your thighs,
graceful guillotines,
have excised
my desire

like a bird in sleep,
I'm defenceless;
prove now
the gentleness of your love

THE LOVER

I

The long shadows are knives
Dividing the day.

At night the sun-rounded edges of snowdrifts
Become ice.

On clear nights
Each edge
Is the Milky Way.

II

So often as angels approach
Is the journey easier:
The sound of guitars,
The voices of my people
Form a canopy
Over the path.
In such closeness
I delight,
My body remembering
Hands,
Their warmth,
Welcome.

THE LOVER (Cont'd.)

III
Life has such weight:
In another skin
I flew,
Delighted in the sun,
The wind that turned the wing of the hawk,
The growing chatter of fledglings.

IV
I welcome iron trees' first laborious strivings
And silver spiles' lymphatic deluge,
The first twig-tip torches
Flickering in the brain of the bee,
Arousing the sleeping genius of dance.

TO INANNA

Were we lovers once?
I have visions of you
Among the sacred trees
Of the Tigris sanctuary:
The walls are washed by the music of waters
Vibrant with golden fish and starlight . . .
And you are reaching,
Not for the moon —
Long before you had possessed that.

And the air is silk-blossomed,
Bursting with psalms
Older than the digging stick
Or the first jewels of maize.

Is it my child you carry? —
Or is it I who curl within,
At once Desired
And Fulfillment of desires
First felt when you arose
From the embrace of the ocean?

AVATAR
— for D.A.E.

a young woman rises in the night
and moves to her child's bed;
her body is smoke in the darkness;
others will never know
until the child is gone

in the precision of the frog's eye,
a beauty beyond labour:
out of the many distresses,
a hand turned in gentleness —
a curve as speaking as light